Send Me a Light

poems by

Julia Gregg

Finishing Line Press
Georgetown, Kentucky

Send Me a Light

Copyright © 2020 by Julia Gregg
ISBN 978-1-64662-262-7 First Edition
All rights reserved under International and Pan-American Copyright Conventions. No part of this book may be reproduced in any manner whatsoever without written permission from the publisher, except in the case of brief quotations embodied in critical articles and reviews.

ACKNOWLEDGMENTS

Thanks to Julia Zave for photos from The Nature Morte Project, to Annie Dixon, and to Gina Ambrosino for the dedication page photo of The Great Georgiana in Brooklyn, NY.

Publisher: Leah Maines

Editor: Christen Kincaid

Cover Art: Images from The Nature Morte Project by Julia Zave

Dedication Page Photo: Gina Ambrosino

Author Photo and Pages 10 and 25: Annie Dixon

Additional Interior Photos: Images from The Nature Morte Project by Julia Zave

Cover Design: Elizabeth Maines McCleavy

Order online: www.finishinglinepress.com
also available on amazon.com

Author inquiries and mail orders:
Finishing Line Press
P. O. Box 1626
Georgetown, Kentucky 40324
U. S. A.

Table of Contents

Send Me a Light 1

Where Light Enters/Fill in the Blank Verse 2

The Envelope 4

Nightfall in Montgomery 5

Of Wisteria and Women 6

Poem for My Brother 7

Glory Days 8

From the Beach, for my son 9

Tennessee 11

Mountain Climb 12

Mobility 13

Twenty-one 15

I Love You in Silence 16

The Deer 17

Light out of Brooklyn 18

November 19

Barrenness 20

Blank Verse #2 21

Perky Yoga Girl 22

Learning Curve 23

Of Tomatoes and Sacred Places 24

Pilgrims 26

Circle Unbroken 28

On This Holy Journey /Catch a Falling Star 29

Morning in St. Helena 30

Work 31

March 32

Sun 33

Shells, Early Evening 34

Olea, True Story 35

A Sign in Blank Verse, Half-Hidden 36

You Girl with the Rope in Your Teeth 37

Grace 39

Prayer 40

Morning Song 41

Evening Song 42

January Sunrise 44

Transformation 45

Love 46

For those who know great loss;
help us each to understand that the circle remains unbroken.

"Our birth is but a sleep and a forgetting..." —William Wordsworth

Send Me a Light

You open the map
in waning light
        that seeps through your windows on DeKalb.
Turn here for the bookstore,
            you say,
                sending me into the after-dusk
                past brownstones that sleep against the curb.
One light flicks on in a window, an image archetypal, dreamlike, safe
                        on this unfamiliar street.

I try to earn the confidence you've draped around me
—that I can find my way and won't be lost.

You're busy. A man with a bar to run.
I'm a mother far from home who finds Brooklyn streets bewildering
until electric sunburst of the Greenlight Bookstore beckons me toward
things I know:
                        books—the same in any city.

What would I give to relive that evening?
You, my grown son, believing in an infallibility I never possessed,
always assuming a strength I'd feigned to make you feel secure,
sending me out alone as if I could do anything.

Did you think I could survive your death
    on the corner of Sixth and Sterling
      (just a mile and three years hence)?
That night on Vanderbilt and DeKalb, was there any clue of what would
come?
No clue.

Send me a light,
—archetypal, angelic
and
I will try to earn the confidence you've draped across my shoulders
—that I can find my way and won't be lost and broken...

  I am lost and broken.

Where Light Enters/Fill in the Blank Verse

Beyond the glass, against the upper pane
   backlit leafless limbs
   of hawthorn twigs
   tangle, twist in wind, far from the roots
   that reach down, grounded in a deeper
                        source.
I turn to ease the ache of lying still;
the dog turns too,
and she reclaims her spot
against the tender bend
          behind my knees.
Give me understanding,
a request
as snowplows pace the pavement of the street,
grinding teeth on asphalt, chomping ice.

Show me the way to fill in all the blanks
of people, places I have been and lost
Briefly I sleep and dream of scented warmth;
camellias drop and I'm a child again
before I knew you'd come to be my son.
  A slant of light (a serving, sliver, slice)
  illuminates the upper window glass...
  And enters where my soul is split in half.

The Envelope

Mystery and memory
consigned to us
for transcription…

We melt the seal
          (like a honeyed wax,
            garden-scented)
that covers
long ago
and far away;
we read it all again
to discover
what has mattered…

Nightfall in Montgomery

1960

In a summer street
of children and bikes
the radio plays *West Side Story*
and we draw hopscotch grids
with chalk

The dusk still lingers
all these years later
—dusk blue and still
  with no wind moving
  across porches
  where bathrobed women
  water
    evening shrubs...

Of Wisteria and Women

The roots went down
into an orange-red morass
(as if the earth had been soft loam);

around unfurling wisps
in sorghum-thick humidity
leaves and fragile blooms
lifted—and against all winds
      they thrived,
their bines like soldered spines.

Roots and stalks
curled in clay
—offering, on the surface,
  coy blossoms
  like lavender scented gloves

to be kissed
    by
        April air…

Poem for My Brother

You
   with your gossamer heart
   hidden
   in its rough-and-tumbled case…
You
   with your pearl and paper heart
   in its barnacled, too-unlikely shell,

Catch our time and call it back
—when life was played in hopscotch moves
  and falls were just for laughs
Hold our time up in your hand
   —until the memory floats away
     like dandelion in wind

You
   there with me laughing
   in the summer egg-shell evening dusk
   in the rose-and-golden almost night,
 Catch our time and call it back
   —until the memory floats away
              like
                        dandelion
                                in wind…

Glory Days

How many October poems
rest in tissued boxes?
Today again
      autumn light lines lace curtains
      sending a sun batik across
      the corner of my page
Springsteen plays
and takes me back to
Glory Days
      when tramps like us
      baby, we were born
             to run...

From the Beach, **for my son**

I take back pictures
that cannot be pressed into frames

They are stilled in time
      (heart pictures)
of you kneeling
—your hands lacing water and sand.

You are safe in the harbor of
 my watching you
and your eyes
  (the color of waves—
   blue and green and brown)
lift to see if I am there.

Always
I will be there...

But
your six-year-old legs
will grow strong and tall
And you will build castles
 (not just in sand)...

You will launch ships
      of your own making
when this child-time has passed.

And so I hold here in my heart
 —where light cannot fade the colors
  or time tear the corners—
this picture of you
 —freckled with sun
  poised at the water's edge—
  peaceful in our harbor time
that comes before the
    launching
        out...

Tennessee

On misty winter chill days
On haze and silver gray days
when ice and leaves—
      brown earthen leaves—
crack and whisper underfoot,
heading home is harboring
and coming in from woodland walks
means mist and silver gray stay
outside in winter chill.

On amber roaring fire days
On spice-tea, warm-your-feet days
When kitchen is the cookie place—
      all toasty warm
      with honey air,
being home is harboring
and coming in from woodland walks
means amber, brown-your-feet time
and spice-tea, honey warmth.

Mountain Climb

The July breeze hurries home across the bridge,
and rubbing its fingers playfully
through flowers planned in hanging pots,
    resting only a moment on my porch,
it then begins its climb
up brown and green hills
home
to cabin windows
    (half gold-plated with five o'clock sun).

Mobility

People on city buses are strong
or broken
Nothing in between.
Faces of anger, defiance,
                resignation
(disembodied
 disheartened)
gaze (glazed) through tinted windows.

Infrequently I ride buses, too,
   usually in silence.

Sometimes I smile
and
then the man with the red, white, and blue bandana says:
"I write poetry."
Encouraged, he recites.

"Nice," I whisper...
but he's not finished.
Another verse
and then another.

He sweats and wipes his face with his American flag.
"Damn Osama bin Laden," he murmurs.

I politely turn away
to face the woman next to me
...cloth bag on her lap
...world's weight in her stare.
I know enough of what she's seen
to admire her gaunt posture,
        her forced strength.

But
then I exit at the stop
...to claim my car and travel

home.
What does it mean to have no way off
or out?

Twenty-one

(for my son)

Manhattan
glare attack
Hunter S. and Kerouac

jazz-rap
deepest night
oozing schmooze
in lamplight

night club
richest blue
liquid walk

    I think of you.

I Love You in Silence

I love you in silence,
missing you across distances too great to span
except in spirit

like Keats' 'gold to airy thinness beat'
my connection to you is ethereal,
a golden umbilical cord
stretched through the ether of intuition.

Science says
that sons conceived half a century ago
leave behind
cells
when they
exit the womb
like a patron's tip
—a twenty percent
gratuity

Somehow I knew that,
   no research needed.
...a resonant cord
emerging like a spider's filament
vibrating across the cosmos...

You laugh in New York City
and the sound rides a tightened string;
you cry
and
I wait
unsettled
for your call.

The Deer

I cannot rinse the picture from my mind
of Sunday afternoon…
the car ahead
colliding with a graceful running deer.

It was gone, no question, in that one moment.

Off into the side woods its
        friend or mate or mother
         moved on alone without it
What else was there to do?

I shiver to remember how it split my heart.

Light out of Brooklyn

About you
they said,
"He had such a light…"
…the refrain in Brooklyn
on that April day when I held on to every word,
touched every friend you knew as if I were touching you…
The stories told, the ways they all loved you, fill part of the
emptiness that waits here for you.

In unexpected moments when the wound is ripped open without warning and
I see your face
        —in other tragedies on the news
        —in plays as the mother holds her dying son…
I say, I did not have that chance
all the while knowing
I could not have borne it.
A saintly stranger, brave enough to approach a death scene,
held your hand as your Soul went out of the world.

I imagine It lifting up above the church at Sixth and Sterling,
rising between buildings to the clear blue
and on into the Light, becoming part of spires and spikes of radiance.

Here today I spread before me the poems written for you in life and after life,
                  —my scraped, raw heart leaking onto the page.

November

The silence, the humidity hang heavy
—a canopy over November.
Raindrops rest distended
        on the spiny fingertips
       on the bony fingertips
 of wet November limbs
          bowing in reverence
         of winter rest to come.

Barrenness

I understand barrenness.
Barrenness of landscape
in winter
Barrenness of spirit
—a horrifying diagnosis, pain, death, disgrace,
any number of things
to leave us
hollow
with gifts that no longer matter;
we are without a rooted place
on this empty edge
with freezing grey skies for as far as we can see.

Blank Verse #2

A blanched white staring existential thought
that we are insignificantly alone
calls forth—at first—a whisper of protest
and then a surer voice begins to lift
from somewhere in a rooted energy.
Thin strands of understanding start to grow
like tendrils toward a light just breaking through,
clues found in love and art, in acts and words
connecting us to something we just glimpse
before the screen goes blank and we fall back.

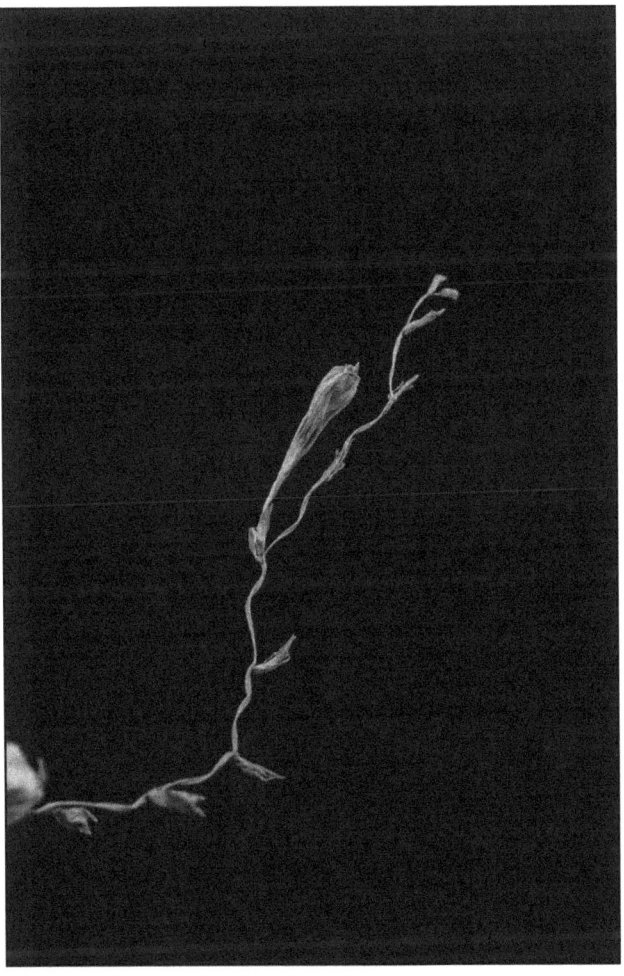

Perky Yoga Girl

She stares at her yoga top in the mirror opposite,
    tugs on her mini-shorts—
but her hair's so cute
I forgive her
    for thinking she's so precious that no rules apply.
Long ago we all felt that way?
I am traveling back to remember...

She moves around the room, mostly instructing those
who have some faint hope of doing a double bind
or wrapping their arms like pretzels.
We were all jaunty once
and dream of being so again,
even though we know
how life bends sun salutations to the ground.

I will not be the sad and embittered woman who has lost elasticity
and a son.
So I bury my face in a child's pose and pray:
Let me remember
and make sense of it all...
help me piece it together.
Gratefulness and understanding, please.
Namaste.

Learning Curve

With the left arm
reaching forward
and the right fist
trailing backward
    (clutching what I've
    left behind),
I stumble again
    through the growing and unfolding
    the blooming and the falling away…
Longer and longer
my limbs and memory stretch—
until
like modeling clay
both grow so long and spindly
that they wrap around the earth,
touching in the middle, encasing a world
that has always felt less like home
than
a cosmic
learning curve…

Of Tomatoes and Sacred Places

We each build shrines in our own ways
—a garden, a book,
  a workshop, a bicycle on the corner of Sixth and Sterling.

We harvest in these holy places
            fruits and remembrance.

We leave flowers and wreaths, poems and pineapples—
Offerings to say

We will never forget.
Come here for gifts
        of our love…

Leave us signs in sacred places
            of presence and peace.

Pilgrims

Years ago
you said you loved
the pilgrim soul in me
and left Yeats on the table
for me to find.

We were young and
beautiful and
open;
who could have known
we would grow so close
to *old and gray and full of sleep...*

In these years
I have closed curtains
over my heart

—at first just sheers,
but later
velvet
pulled across. Closed.

I am a private actor,
—a dancer in solitude
            less given to share.

But
you come again
and throw back
one by one the layers
so that
shyly at first but surely
we are
moving
trusting
laughing
   in sunlight

    and stage light
—scrims askew—
pilgrims, partners in this play that writes itself

as if no time has passed.

Circle Unbroken

This morning
in a round basket
   of needles, threads
   of odds and ends
that belonged first to my mother
             and then to me,
I unfolded a random paper
torn, stained and
holey
with elementary lettering:
#422 Name Tag
    Send $1.75 & Bazooka comics to:
    Bazooka, Box 7860, Westbury, N.Y.
                      11582
God
how I miss the little boy who wrote
with such innocence,
knowing whatever he wanted
would come to him…

In this sanctified spring season
erratic, stained and
holy
send me signs
Lord,
by and by
of circles that remain
      unbroken…

On This Holy Journey/Catch a Falling Star

A stranger from an opposite coast sends an unexpected note:
'I hope this is not out of your wheelhouse
but I was told to send you a message and I am here.

'He wanted me to tell you he is okay
and he is happy
and he is around
and misses
and loves you.'

Make of it what you will,
but I will say what I have known:
One Catholic counselor who communes with
 saints and angels,
Two swishes that cannot be explained,
Threes repeating everywhere…
Four mystics, telling secret truths,
Five lights flickering without cause.

I have seen one flaming star
fall right before my window—
and knowing it was for me,
I caught the glow of it
just as the song instructs
because
   on this holy journey
   filled with huge mysteries, regrets, and losses,
   only a few great loves flicker and persist

and I will need this Light
to warm me on my way…

Morning in St. Helena

Sycamore
   (chameleon lime and dusty brown)
 sifts through window screen
 under a slanted sun
              that slides
                         across September
                                  like a scarf.
The very air's a gift
so thin and clear,
I take a sip;
mourning climbs out to
meet morning
and I find that I can
breathe again...

Work

> *"Work is love made visible…"* –Kahlil Gibran

In this workshop
of writers
with hair mopping their foreheads
(two with caps)

tentative eyes
imagine,
stop and
stare.

All
bend over paper, pad, and pen
tapping out tone and mood like
Morse code,
sending signals that scrape the scabs off
scars and secrets
until sparks start
to cauterize
   the wounds.

March

I'm waiting
for the oldest week in winter
to die into spring

for the fat, hot buttercup bud
to burst to yellow,
                      defying frost,
                        burning it to droplets that
                            slip down slithery infant leaves
                              slide down stems and
                                  send up watery, worshipping
                                        vapor hands
                            petitioning…

and accepting.

Sun

Crossing 30-A
when morning leaks across the sand,

sniffing out coffee
when the sun first curves across the sign
at Seagrove Market,

passing Thyme
where oak groves
wrap me in early light and shade
        —first one and then the other,
          like cloak and boa
            slinking down my back—

I thread my way along the coast
like a mist that
lifts above a peaceful turquoise gulf…
and understand
I have not come for water
but for light…

Shells, Early Evening

I have gathered
a dozen tiny shells,

one so small
that it clings
to the dime
      resting orphaned
      at the bottom
      of my cup.

I had expected more.

Spread against the sill,
in late afternoon sun,
one breaks and one is lost

So this is what remains:
nuanced shades and shapes
      of ten tiny shells,
beautiful ample harvest
is what I choose
to whisper.

Olea, True Story

Three years:
this long it has taken me
to lift all defenses against crumbling
and see you
there
again,
in Olea
   (exotic cafe on a classic Brooklyn Street)
in your perfect white shirt
simply
pulling out your chair;

across from you,
my pride and love emanate so brightly
that the restaurant dims
its lights.

A Sign in Blank Verse, Half-Hidden

From edge of woods in summer's idling dusk
a deer appears; its eyes lock in with mine

I think: So you've come back to me in stealth
            —like some old friend or guide from ageless time
to comfort and leave remedy or hope,
half-hidden in the gloaming
            and the leaves

You Girl with the Rope in Your Teeth

Only a shard of white glass moon
and two stars traveling on either side of it
pass in this dark sky that should be dawning.

The clock sings seven, and still no sun.

Who is this person,
waiting in my chair by the window
finally without a rope held in her mind-teeth,
anxiously tugging
belated light across the sky?
When did she relinquish control of jobs not in her sphere?

Oh, the agony of being in charge of it all,
dropping all mistakes and regrets
into buckets labeled 'Failures'
each time the weather, the outcome, the decision
isn't right.

I am leaving you behind,
you girl with the rope in your teeth.
I'm putting aids on my eyes and ears and heart
to observe...

Hafiz wrote:
This place where you are right now,
God circled on a map for you.

What place?
This city?
This chair by the window?
This emotional space, this port-of-call?
Let it be.

Just now a pink line divides the ground from
a bluing sky

All in good time:
this view,
this poem,
this dawn…

Grace

Sometimes
the grace of a place
    appears to end

and we take our love and lessons
like luggage
to a different
        pinpoint
        on the horizon
to another slant of sun.

Sometimes
the sadness of a place ends, too.

One morning before full light
    the outline of a cardinal
      (where no red bird has been before)
sounds a signal note
to say that singing survives
            and circles do not end
            nor love
            nor grace
            nor mystery.

Prayer

I have seen your calling cards;

on a hawk's wing you have come
so close
I had to think to breathe.

Still I implore:

Do not lose patience with me;
visit me in dreams and prayers,
   in neon orbs
   in trembling lights
   in swishes and
   in silence.

I want to keep both worlds'
mysterious acquaintance
until I understand.

Morning Song

The rain shines
in lamplight that settles
across the stairs.

An old injury
from back to leg to foot whispers
in damp darkness
as I climb
to sing my
morning song:

Let me keep one foot
on these stairs
and one foot in the Light
until I get this right.

Evening Song

The last of evening
curls across lilies
left long past their time
in crystal vases.

Faded,
they have lost their youth and yet
in age
they are exquisite still
—the delicate curve toward the window
—the ridges, like finely creased skin
—rising from a shored up core from which all else unfurls…

January Sunrise

Seeking peace,
we shuffle through last year's leaves
on this solitary stroll

(my dog and I seem one in quiet purpose,
though who can know for sure…)

We trample across all things fallen
that snap and break,
brown beneath our feet—

Five minutes pass in quiet
before the
squirrels send warnings
in the half-light
from limbs above us

Ten minutes more:
children, listening for the bus,
prance an icy dance
to music from across the way
where
workers turn up radios
and
Latin music beats in time
to hammering

Everything comes alive
anew
in this
January sunrise,
blue and pink as a baby's cradle—

Transformation

I have gathered all soulmates
in the curve of my hand
(like a flower)
and held them all against my heart
for just this moment.

They will scatter again into air,
back to jobs and loves,
—to other choices they have made

but
we are joined at the
Spirit
and the Light between us holds
despite all that falls away from us,
through any shifts in form.

Love

Love follows
everywhere—
city to city
life into death
from this plane to the next

Love leaps into the mystery
because
what choice does it have?

You will know Love;
it does not
pretend
or give up
or fade out
or go home.

Even when it seems
alone,

it waits
    Connected.

Julia Zave's photographs have appeared in *VOGUE, The New York Times, Forbes, Entrepreneur* and more. She volunteers with Pixie Park and CoachArt in the Bay Area where she lives. The floral photographs in *Send Me a Light* are a part of her Nature Morte Project, a collection exploring "the slow decay of flowers, their limited lifetime in one form, their physicality, structure and essence. In each, the mystical and physical worlds come together; their lifestream continues as their form evolves."

Julia Hightower Gregg is a writer and educational consultant who lives in Indiana. She was a columnist for the *Evansville Courier and Press* for almost three decades, as well as a founding member of Signature School in Evansville where she taught Advanced Placement and International Baccalaureate English. *Wild Sweet Orange Ride* was her first book, published by Vineyard Stories in 2014, and *Threads*, a children's story, was her second book, published in 2016. She holds a BS from Auburn University, an MS from Peabody College of Vanderbilt University, and an MFA from Murray State University.

Send Me a Light is her first book of poetry, compiled after the death of her only child in 2016. The collection, meant to extend empathy and hope to others who are grieving, attempts to make sense of the way a life unfolds, concluding that only kindness matters and only love survives.

www.ingramcontent.com/pod-product-compliance
Lightning Source LLC
Chambersburg PA
CBHW042145160426
43201CB00022B/2413